The Wit and Wisdom of Anonymous

Clay Bridges
PRESS

The Wit and Wisdom of Anonymous
Copyright © 2024

Published by Clay Bridges Press in Houston, TX
www.ClayBridgesPress.com

All rights reserved. No part of this publication may be reproduced, stored in a retrieval system, or transmitted in any form by any means, electronic, mechanical, photocopy, recording, or otherwise, without the prior permission of the publisher, except as provided for by USA copyright law.

Unless otherwise indicated, scripture quotations are taken from the Holy Bible, New Living Translation, copyright ©1996, 2004, 2015 by Tyndale House Foundation. Used by permission of Tyndale House Publishers, Carol Stream, Illinois 60188. All rights reserved.

ISBN: 978-1-68488-113-0 (Hardback)
ISBN: 978-1-68488-111-6 (Paperback)
eISBN: 978-1-68488-112-3

Special Sales: Most Clay Bridges titles are available in special quantity discounts. Custom imprinting or excerpting can also be done to fit special needs. Contact Clay Bridges at Info@ClayBridgesPress.com

"Out of the same mouth proceed blessing and cursing."
James 3:10a

"Truthful words stand the test of time ..."
Proverbs 12:19

This book is dedicated to all those unnamed people who have given voice to wit and wisdom which has been and will be enjoyed by many. Their souls produced these nuggets of truth that reached across the ages to encourage other anonymous people. They aren't rock stars, sports stars, movie stars or sit in seats of power. Their power emerges from the thoughts they have shared, although no one may remember their names. Their silence is broken. Enjoy their wit and wisdom.

One further note. If the author has inadvertently included a quote which has in fact been given attribution to another in print please let us know and we will do our best to correct our error.

Enjoy *The Wit and Wisdom of Anonymous*

Embrace the *privilege* of *responsibility.*

BASED ON II CORINTHIANS 8:4

When I am in *Your presence* my only response should be *praise.*

ASAP
As Soon As Provided

May Platitudes
and Pontifications
fueled by Pride
be
Plowed under by Prayer
and Petitions
under-girded by Praise.

YTD
Yield to Death

Faith *Flounders* in the FAMILIAR;

Faith *Flourishes* in the FIRE.

ADD
Adoration Deficit Disorder

Clostrofibia

—

when one gets
in a tight spot he lies.

STG

Saved To Give,

Grow, and Glorify

The thing that moves me from
<u>understanding faith</u>
and
<u>trust to living them</u>
is testing.

May my service be extended
based on what
others stand to gain
—
not what I imagine
I may lose.

Our strongholds and idols
will be destroyed
and left in the wake of revival

———————

it will go through them,
not around them.

In your act of service, keep your *heart in it* and your *hands off of it.*

Our sufferings
are sandwiched between
God's mercies and
His comfort.

BASED ON II CORINTHIANS 1:3

To disobey is to be
POWERLESS.

Use me, Lord,
until I go,
or
You come.

A hunter often returns home with a broken *hart.*

If something smells fishy,
hold your *knows*.

The impatient man says,
"Lift this *wait*
from my shoulders."

The *goodness of another* can sometimes blind us to the gravity of their sin.

P4
Persistently, Powerfully, and Prayerfully Patient

We are in the most danger
when we keep You at a safe distance.

We are not to be
reservoirs of blessings
but a
sprinkler system
through which
blessings flow
out to others.

It's one thing for the
world to live Flesh First,
Soul Second,

but quite another
for a Christian to do so.

PEACE

Patiently Enduring All Catastrophes and Encounters

The physical pain we experience as we near the transition from this life to the next are birth pangs.

C3
Constantly and Confidently Content

Obedience is the place where *"have to"* and *"want to"* should intersect.

As a child of God,
you are <u>always</u>
in the
Promised Land.

RCA

* * *

Repent, Commit, Abide

―

Naughty behavior
results in
knotty problems

―

Absence
makes the heart
WONDER.

Absence
makes the heart
WANDER.

When faced with a knotty
conscience call

* * *

WWMS
WHAT WOULD MOTHER SAY.

Don't obsess
over not being #1

———

even the greatest orchestras
in the world
have second fiddles.

When a hungry squirrel
drops an acorn,
he loses a meal,
and his descendants gain a home.

* * *

Think long term.

Me, me, me, me
is not just a vocal exercise,
it's also a
philosophy of life.

A half-truth
is like a
COFFIN

———

both are
surrounded
by dirt.

Idle
too long
before a
temptation,
and it
becomes
an
IDOL.

Unaddressed temptations are like termites

———

they eat away at your foundation.

I,
for one,
prefer antisocial distancing

Retirement during the
Coronavirus pandemic

---

shelved in place.

Introverts
help
extroverts
do things excellently.

The difference between
<u>back up</u> and <u>back down</u>
is that the first one entails
reconsideration
while the second one is
retreat.

* * *

Try the first one first;
the second one may or may not
then be the right option.

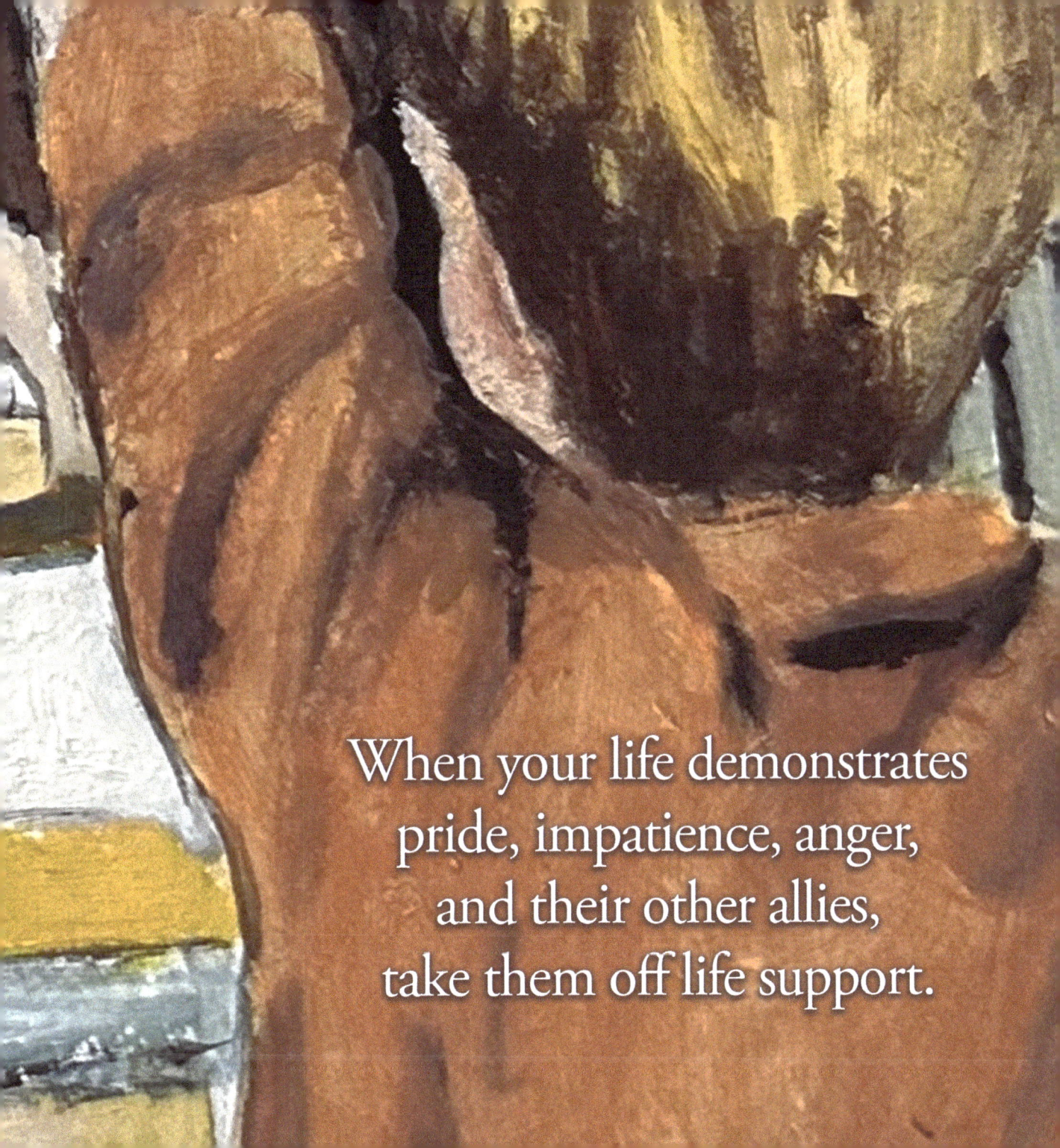

A market containing *strange* and *unusual* trinkets is a **bizarre bazaar.**

Large African antelope decoys

are

fake gnus.

Toss 'N Turn

∗ ∗ ∗

the TNT that blows up
a night's rest.

Shrink Wrap
a hug from a psychiatrist

The only gray matter
an old fool has
is in his
hair follicles.

Don't let a
BAD ATTITUDE
be a backseat driver to
OBEDIENCE.

The big C is
Christ,
not cancer.

Fear Him,
not it.

PRAYER

the power tool of choice

for sons of the *Carpenter.*

QUIT *wresting* with another, and START *resting* with contentment.

www.ingramcontent.com/pod-product-compliance
Lightning Source LLC
Chambersburg PA
CBHW061409090426
42740CB00024B/3478